Iron Mountain Road

Iron Mountain Road

EAMONN WALL

Iron Mountain Road

SALMON POETRY

Published in 1997 by
Salmon Publishing Ltd,
Cliffs of Moher, Co. Clare

A catalogue record for this book is available from the British Library.

Salmon Publishing gratefully acknowledges the
financial assistance of the Arts Council.

ISBN 1 897648 85 5 Softcover
ISBN 1 897648 69 3 Hardcover

Cover design by Estresso
Set by Siobhán Hutson
Printed by Redwood Books, Kennet Way, Trowbridge, Wiltshire

for Matthew and Caitlin Wall

Acknowledgements

Some of the poems included in this collection have appeared in *Blue Canary, Crab Orchard Review, Cúirt Journal, Éire-Ireland, Here's Me Bus, Nebraska Review*.

The material in italics in *Yellow Band* is from the Mark Rothko information sheet at the Sheldon Memorial Gallery, University of Nebraska-Lincoln. The sheet was prepared by the Sheldon's Curator of Education, Karen Janovy.

oh god it's wonderful
to get out of bed
and drink too much coffee
and smoke too many cigarettes
and love you so much

Frank O'Hara

Contents

One

Two

Three

One

Four Stern Faces/South Dakota

I was living in a bedsit in Donnybrook
when John Lennon was shot outside the
Dakota apartment building in New York City
and that's what I'm thinking this morning
piloting my family through the hollow
darkness on Iron Mountain Road, trespassing
on the holy ground of the Lakota nation.

Four stern faces in the distance address
me and when I get stuck after rattling off
Washington & Lincoln I call on Matthew to
fill in the blanks and wonder how the hell
will I pass the civics test when I apply
for citizenship. I could tell you all
about Allen Ginsberg & Adrienne Rich
but presidents, state capitols and amendments
to the constitution would snooker me, and
I get the feeling the I.N.S. doesn't care
too much for postmodern American poetry.
Caitlin belongs to the woods – mosses,
pine needles, slow moving light and shade,
a bright face in the back of the car
breathing a fantastic language, this
slow mid-morning pilgrimage I drive
my loved ones forward and climbing.

When Lennon was dying I was typing
the forms to come to America: on this
journey through the Sandhills – Irish sand

dunes without the sea – to the Black Hills
to wild flowers with names so gorgeous
I cannot bear to hear you say them.
Native people, 'Strawberry Fields Forever,'
Ryan White dying in Indiana. My children
craving this just as the matchsticks and
cats' eyes on the Gorey road mesmerised them,
howling now for lunch. Here the light is
different, the evenings shorter, Gods are weeping.

And there's no escape from caring or
from history: to lie on high plains,
prairie grasses, and Black Hills is to
be blown into their stories, drowned in
their summer rains. Just when I think I've
lost the Irish rings around the tree, I open
the door and find red clay stuck on the
tyres, the whole earth screaming, my children
breathing on the electric hairs above my collar.

Being woken one ordinary workday to Lennon
being dead, 'Imagine' on the radio, remembering
the grown-ups weeping in late November '63,
one morning in Dublin when it finally struck
that heroes are flowers constantly dying on
these black and holy hills we spend the years
wandering towards till light reveals a universe
beyond stony victorious faces bolted to a rock.

Freewheeling By the Platte River: A Song

When I woke this Wednesday your hair
was spread on the pillow like the
many channels of the Platte River.

As I drive westward with the trucks
into the absence of trees, corn, cuts
in the horizon, I fix on the browned
grass flecked with the end of snow,
on those signs of our ageing into
the life of the prairie in winter –
this cloister of *Diet Coke*, draws,
artificial creamer for your coffee,
and too much country 'n western on
the radio. At night you roll against
me for my warmth. I trace from the
backs of your knees to your highest
vertebrae the cities of this state
from Omaha all the way to Chadron.
You turn towards me trusting in these
warming motions naming grasses
awakening the soil to the secrets
you have come to plant. The Land
The Land you sing straw hat on
your knees and yes I have heard it
talk to you and the Platte River
calls your name to me this afternoon
and I imagine you shin-deep and skirts
raised dancing on a shallow bar
in the middle of the flowing.

When I woke this Wednesday your hair
was spread on the pillow like the
many channels of the Platte River.

Father, Father

Having crawled through
the tiled catacombs under
the Port Authority. Heard

balls clattering behind
glass, check-it-out merchants

but Isaac Bashevis Singer dead
was the word on the street.

Stalled buses. Traffic lights
stuck on yellow, brownies
hugging meters, the *Newsday*
sign shattered on the sidewalk,
the national debt headstone
flickering, a mocking pulse,
Girls, Girls, Girls, The
Croissant Shop, the
New York Public Library
Bryant Park, sauerkraut and
smoke from the vendor's carts.

You liked buildings with
courtyards like mine and

hearing your dead language
spoken in diners on Columbus Avenue.

I don't care much about my
dead language except the
poems of Nuala Ní Dhomhnaill,
the cúpla-focail-merchants
killed the Irish lingo,
but, Father Singer,
I know what you mean.

The immigrant has witnessed two worlds
this much is true, the immigrant writer

is the witness' memory who pens lines
full of shame, lines full of hope.

Our leader has fallen. Our leader is dead.

Driving to Kearney, Nebraska

We were slumped under nicotined photos
of old men in Kehoe's of St. Anne St. A

morning in a hotel room undressing again
hearing someone push a brush across a

floor, a car backfire, and a faint
presence of the tide. Rostrevor, Co.

Down. Out today's window machinery rusts
at the edge of a field: summer brought

the best out of us travelling downhill
from Equamville to clanking boats in

Honfleur harbour. I remember you looking
impatiently for the sun describing

your father's world to me. Athenry,
County Galway. It is difficult

to keep love going, a bare landscape
spins on sixteen wheels 3000 miles

from the sea, and the past is as
bright as wounds opened by Hank

Williams's songs on the radio.
Driving to Kearney, Nebraska

into the eye of a once mighty sea.

Warm & Fastened

Around each corner whitewash
pebbledash or wet concrete

smoking chimneys announce
words alive among mothers
hearing radios together

the dead in the graveyards
and geldings poking faces
add layers to each day.

I can't walk out into a
wilderness to cook & fish:
humans will declare that

we gave up outdoor cooking
centuries ago. Are you a
foreigner or a Yank?

At twilight, I'll see
the *Harp* sign in Kennedy's
a mile down the hillside

on open roads each dog-and-stick-man
knows my name and business.

No wilderness:
no way to get away
from electric light and sing-song voices

with each day ditches and mounds move
nearer: one evening on dew-anointed
grass I'll waken: warm and fastened.

Farm Aid

The colours do not merge according
to the sun. The quilt is stable, as
I was taught the shapes of shells
& stones on beaches my hands explain
textures of soils and grasses, and
hear what torments the winds carry
from dying farms, truckloads of
families on the final trips to town.
This evening potatoes boiling,
salad made, the roast cooling I hear
Fr. Jones saying prayers for the corn,
and oats and barley in Star of the
Sea church in Riverchapel, County
Wexford. Returned from our drive we
listen to the Farm Aid concert on the
radio, children with crayons at my
feet dividing vast sheets of paper
into enormous Nebraska fields of
soy beans and corn. Immortal farm
families, enormous tombs on each
horizon, a wailing absence of young voices.

Ardamine, Co. Wexford

Gas lamps burn in the caravans
on the borough. In bed I hear 'The
Hucklebuck' from the Tara Ballroom
and after 'The Soldier's Song'
the sea whispering, whisper-
ring ... ering, 'Stop firing stones,'
'I'll race you to the rocks.'

Reverie: The Dublin – Rosslare Train

I'm travelling home for the weekend from Connolly
    thinking of Philip Casey's poem
about returning to Gorey 'a voice rises faintly over the
    beach as the train'
in *The Year of the Knife* which reminds me I should phone
    to thank him for
the dinner he paid for while I was talking on the street
    the other evening
and I pass through Westland Row where I got on and
    off as a student in Dublin.
I see my mother in her sunchair with a cup of tea and
    a fag – the Irish kind –
hearing the gaggle of children mine included and then
    nothing but the wash wash
of the waves over the stones, over the shells, onto the
    sands in the
middle of summer and I know what she doesn't hear –
    sunlight tweaking the apex
of a wave – is part of the heartache of the years we
    have shared. My father
with his shears merrily clipping the silly edges of the
    buckthorn thinking of
a swim and a cup of tea. And I'm in Dublin for six
    weeks with students full of
ideas and silliness knowing it all will end, that I'll
    know when to stop.
Again to be lying down with you again in County
    Wexford, to promise you again
all I've promised before, most recently in Spain. Our
    children hollering
at the birds asleep in bed covered to necks in quilts for
    the Irish summer

which isn't getting any better, and I'll stroke their
    heads with my travelled hands
till the swallows have gone to the roofs of the trees,
    and their breathings slow.
This is a poem for you, reader, to pass the time as you
    go like me to home
from home and if my journey confuses you, I hear you,
    your mind ticking over
as you head towards Galway or Westport to stations full
    of beating hearts.
To travel and arrive: anticipate and see in twilight the
    lights of the town
in the late wind in July in Ireland. And if you know this
    train I'm on
you won't miss the markers through the window. Bray
    Station where *The Miracle*
is set – better than *The Crying Game* in my opinion –; the
    Irish Sea to
your left all the way to Wicklow; then the woods and the
    FERT and the Arklow
Van Morrison sings about in *Veedon Fleece*; Paul Funge's
    Gorey Arts Centre
Gorey; and Enniscorthy where I get off Katherine
    Proctor's view of the misty
Slaney. This line is yours and mine, your loves are mine.
    The poem you put
in your bag this morning is this poem, the one you carried
    to the office and
station is this poem. What you think of on the bus to
    Cork or Carrickmacross
is what I write as I glide through the stations of suburban
    Dublin. For eight
years I rode the subways in New York with the faces and
    the tiles outside

here white houses and Barna buildings with luminous
   families passing food
around kitchen tables, fathers like myself freed for the
   weekend. And I
remember last year driving from Omaha, Nebraska, to
   Custer, South Dakota,
thinking as I saw the Nebraska Sandhills for the first time
   that I was once
again in Ireland. Low hills, tufts of grass and if
   I keep on
driving I'll hit the sea somewhere between Courtown and
   Cahore. The children
in the back singing along to Mary Chapin Carpenter and
   Dwight Yoakam
on the radio, and you sunken into your seat dreaming of
   waters I cannot
imagine. Your country, Indian Bride, your long black
   hair blowing towards me.
But I shouldn't be thinking of such things I remind
   myself as I drive this
car. What would the State Patrol make of such an excuse
   for a family
in the ditch? What would the insurance agent say to two
   cars totalled in one year?
Never take chances with foreign born Irish. We have
   been travelling together.
I will approach you under the rusty roofs as the bands
   play on across town.
You are not air. You are memory and rekindled fire
   waiting among your books,
and your herbs, and your children all week for me.
   Such are our days,

such are our years. Unforgettable, we know, as we go
    along exploring our holy
and sacred grounds. In Custer, South Dakota, I imagined
    us sleeping under blankets
in the forest, the candles on the pines transformed into
    clear winter stars.
In the campsite, each rental cabin was named after an
    American president
and I told the clerk that anyone but Nixon, Reagan, or
    Bush would do
to which you added Andrew Jackson, so she gave us
    Kennedy because she was
dull and on account of my nationality. Days when we
    trespassed on the
holy ground of the Lakota nation, when the ancient
    spirits within these hills
sent a buffalo to us on the red dirt road we drove
    to block the
way, to insist you must turn round, you must retreat,
    you have to now
go home rocking Inter-City to County Wexford on the
    oldest rolling stock in
Western Europe, fields crowded with sheep and cows,
    and the slow rivers.
Days coming back like racing clouds, where the reverie
    begins in County
Wexford where 'landscape,' as Philip Casey says, 'gives
    back memories'
...and 'implacably the rails connect the coastal towns.'
    My women are
in Wexford waiting for me. And Wexford is the strong
    inland town and
Wexford is the swoosh, swoosh Irish sea. Women,
    O women.

Two

The Waves, The Waves

It's five o'clock in November in the final
final hour of light in the large prairie sky, this

morning the first frost on the roofs I watched roll
into the gutters and drain onto the concrete pathways

where no one walks. A neighbour says each day
without ice and snow will make the winter shorter and

so I try to be an optimist too. The weather it matters,
it doesn't matter. Tomorrow at dinner I'll say

that I saw the Irish sky in late October, the tree
branch on the sand, the sunken boulders, and Uncle Paddy

on a towel counting heads bobbing on the water. Driving
home I trained my eyes on a falling wave, scrunching

stones and ebb and flow, his white sideburns and navy hat.
I was there again at season's end – the climbing

car, you don't believe it's there until you see it
slate blue and wilder now. But the sea again.

Listen, she whispers. Listen. Last month and
years ago. Nothing ever changes, everything changes

too much. On these quiet Nebraska streets you hear
your heart beat, when you drive west the prairie sky

19

becomes the sea. With my beads (Red Willow People &
Catholic), snow shovel, and radial tyres I'm ready

for the winter. Spring – red red evening on a backroad
the radio plays the children to sleep gently swaying

eternities of corn on this uncertain journey home. Kiss
me on the prairie. Kiss me on the beach. Summer bride.

Sandhills

Walking the verges that skirt
RT. 20 in Northwest Nebraska
through the dunes beyond the
14th fairway into the Irish Sea.

Barbed wire frames these hills
no flap-flap or children's
howling but winds calling out
Lie down, roll across the sands.

Friends, Landscapes, & Life Stories

Judy Highhorse says wearing steel-toed boots she hunts
rattlesnakes in the fields which go for miles on land
her father owns not far from Valentine in Cherry County.

On the top of Ardamine cliff I dig elbow-deep in sand
tar and fields shut out but the sea whose uncertain
colours I raise my eyes forever momentarily to grasp,

and we meet in the Dundee Foodmarket to talk about our
animals and children, to speak some words about America.
Sagebrush and buckthorn, mothers, fathers, and the dead.

Belongings with Attitude

Says the Toaster:
'I was bought in the
Sears in Yonkers &
I'm proud to be
American made –
Slide your bagel into me.'

And the sofa answers:
'So what, pal,
I'm a Jennifer Convertible,
think of all the things
you can do on me –
Watch TV
Roll me out
Drink a cup of Earl Grey Tea.'

'No one moves to Nebraska,'
moans the air conditioner, 'and
we didn't let on where we wuz
headed for. I told a friend
I'd been sent up the river.'

Says the the kitchen table bought
in the Dominican furniture place on
Vermileya St. 'You got more room
now – upstairs and downstairs.
I've always lived in apartments,
and the subway don't rumble
this house. People are so polite
I think I'm gonna go crazy.'

And a kitchen chair butts in:
'Remember me I'm the chair
you flung in the trash room.
I was rescued by the Super,
Mr Rigo, but didn't like the
smell of garlic so I chased
you down. And, Hey, I could
do with a shine and an ice-
cold *Heineken* from a paper
bag. Ya know what I'm sayin',
and I see ya still got that
crappy TV stand ya found
outside the co-op on
Academy St. I hear that lady
died and her stuff is all
dispersed, and I want to know
how come there ain't no live
furniture on the streets of
Omaha, Nebraska, for a citizen to
bring home? Ain't this a city?'

And the old blue lazy
chair replies: 'a fire burns
this evening & our children
lean on their elbows on the
hearth seeing corn float across
prairies like waves across the sea:
eyes large as headlights, hearts
like winter squirrels' barely beating.'

Says the mangy yellow lamp to the old
blue lazy chair: 'Shut up, please,
you're beginning to sound like a
motherfuc – Oh I better not say
it since this ain't New York –
like a dang 'Dairy Queen' ice-cream,
but I gotta say,
I gotta say,
gotta say,
gotta say,

I just can't bring myself to admit it....'

The Westward Journey

Setting out on the westward journey
with eight suitcases and two cats.
On this last night we sleep at the
La Guardia Marriott to swim in the pool,
and begin the busy work of forgetting
Mr. Pedro's large hands stuck in the
till as his fingers float among the
pennies. 'You are leaving New York
to live in America,' he says. 'I would
be afraid of that, and the little ones
will lose their Spanish.' At the end of
the street each Sunday morning bright
speedboats race for the early shadows
under the George Washington Bridge.

I have stored away your cries of
being born: from these ugly streets,
red paint on the old benches in
Payson Playground, to the sweet
brown eyes of an immigrant from
Galicia fumbling and cursing quietly
about for our change. My own childhood
unimaginable without the Slaney humming
'Son, you breathe' as I read the clock
each morning above Louis Kerr's shop.
Impossible that there was another life.

Tonight, my children are singing in the
water at the prospect of a plane ride to
another life, but someone must remember,
there must be someone to write this down.

Night, Night

Night, night
a town and family, I hear

a song across the Market Sq.
past Dunnes Stores and out
into the country wet fields

a solitary voice breaks the
silence and is now the night
to you I turn for confirmation
your even breathing and thin
feather-like fingers. Love is
forever, as they say.

Such a joy to be awake
to be alive in summertime
my daughter's strokes in
the water today this
breeze off the river my
son's flailing at waves
and roaring voice

Night, night
a town and family, I hear.

Blue Light

Because at some stage you must climb those spackled steps
to enter the cool blue light.

Behind you – coiling stainless steel, a swimming pool
and the freeway.

Yellow pad on your knees, you will have to say – I am open
now – foxglove or rose?

Who will be present to hear you breathe?

In a blue church under a beige sky a blind priest reads the
beatitudes beautifully

the late afternoon is covered deep in yesterday's snow.

You have come out of this white day all used-up
and flaked as your neighbour's rusted Ford

wrecked by the length of the journey.

You remember another man who raised his arms
and said that Jesus calls us home

you remember making damp rounds of walks
surrounding a Rathfarnham retreat house,

& running fingers on a holly leaf which felt still like
polished leather

how you looked that season beyond vague evergreens to
the bay from which emerged fish & smokestacks &
     circling planes.

In the blue light a woman in a country 'n western song is
called home. Her eyes fixed on the road, she has money
     for gasoline and cigarettes.

You remember salmon and geese. Wanderers and rivers.
How in your father's village tables are set. A car pulls in
across the street at Cowman's to have its tank filled.

By six, the high windows are bleached of their colour.
The building bright enough for sketching, a winter
evening fallen on the white ground, on the fast-deep
     Missouri River
tunneling headlong for St. Louis, New Orleans, the Gulf.

Bodysurfing

Each route out reveals
one borderline snaking
stream-like by wet ground
and simple winter maples

one plot each single family
home. To have been trained
to walk no further, to be
returned each evening with
just one story gleaned from
a single section of the day.

The other day I bodysurfed
across the crowd to your
knees & walking to the beach
one Thursday afternoon:
woman's voice, brown oils,
crystal, smoky bar and beer
as it was one evening after
five when I swam out from
Ardamine to know the salty
healing of the sea on my
raw, sunburned shoulders.

Father and Daughter: Nebraska

My daughter's dancing at the
back door to the falling snow
picking up her rhythm I sway
from too tight-fitted western
boots and feel a sharp new
loneliness under high clouds
frosted tree branches in
Nebraska. Take it all away and
left will be shadows of trees,
ice & snow, birdseed,
a dancing child.

          If I place
my hands on your shoulders,
you'll stop dancing.

          Naked in
Nebraska without a paper
coffee cup, Uptown mothers
ring-a-roseying in the sun,
& I've moved around too much
opening the blinds at daylight
to search calm streets for
the view I've left behind me.
Blue-jeaned girl, barretted hair,
you are all I have – snow and ice,
trees and music – everything else
fell from the back of a Mayflower
truck somewhere between here and

there, reported to the police,
items considered lost, all
covered by insurance.
And shadows.

            Snow brings
the children out. The world
feels good. Where were you hiding?
Why were your streets so quiet?
I bleed with the dry winter
air a thin blood, a paint-
flecked face, cream by an
upstairs mirror.

            Darling,
I say, sweetheart and angel,
let's go driving just me and
you and we'll stop at Baskin-
Robbins on the way home to
eat – you a Party Cone, me one
scoop of vanilla – to watch
snow ploughs on Underwood
Avenue, and hold hands.

Junk Food

The pumpkins are piled in a trailer
outside the 74 St. Albertson's, the
kids waiting in the car for happy meals
to appear through Window 2 of Burger
King – the fading October light, blowing
leaves, the ugliness of Dodge St. west
of 72nd makes me want to cry, and the
song on the radio is so good it makes
me want to cry, but the children are
so happy with their disgorged bags &
Cokes it makes me want to say a prayer
and drive around again to order a bunch of
whoppers and my son reminds me of the
first time I drove into a fast-food
joint when I 37 seven years of age I
didn't know you had to order at the
metal hole in the wall and drove
straight up to the window and told the
greasy kid what I wanted and he couldn't
believe I didn't know the etiquette of
ordering and that was the Mickey Dees on
Dodge so now I stick to the Home of the
Whopper across the street.

                              I know I'm
slow – I was 28 before I learned how to
ride a bike and that was due to the fact
that (as the NYPD says) I was on the Aran
Islands where there is no public transport-
ation system. You have to turn the radio

down to hear yourself when you order
junk food and the greasy parrot always
shouts it back to you and when you have
an accent it takes a few tries to
get it right. But you see the children's
faces in the back of the car and
you drive on envious because it's
so fucking hard to find pleasure
in the simple things nowadays.

Soon
we'll be buying pumpkins, cutting
horrible faces, burning candles
and the neighbourhood will be full
of magical stories, milk and
pumpkin pie and the snows will
follow and they will sled and I
will shovel & whistle and
parallel play before cooking
some dinner but it won't be junk
food because I can't cook that good.

A Piece of Beautiful Jade

I

I sit at the foot of the stairs hearing music
across town, my children leaping salmon-like

among the dancers, more fine days promised for the
farmers whose strawberry-laden trailers line Island

Road. Tomorrow I'm selling my beat-up Penguins, so
I can rise like the healed man, find the bandstand

and sing & dance with young lovers in late night
quiet corners of Enniscorthy, this Strawberry

Fair, this single summer. How many in a lifetime?
I remember as a teenager sitting on a stout

box by the machinery yard seeing women dance before
a campfire to a lone guitar, to a voice as mesmeric
as it was off-key. How many roads must a man walk down?

Did Noah take his books onto the Ark? His television &
VCR? His Grateful Dead CDs and Sony Walkman? And blue

Blockbuster card? And health club membership which
promised eternal life? His espresso maker and Starbuck's
mug? His heirloom love seat & best blue Wedgewood?

II

The years of reading were rounded out to ninety quid.
Outside by the garage sunflowers have grown to nine feet,

bluegrass rooted in black earth grows as we breathe
and sleep, the great river a few miles away, and all around

the city the silence of land and utility poles. In a dream,
I am on a corner tossing books from a bag – too heavy to

carry home – like a farmer flinging seed. When his
burlap sack is empty, he carries the memory of that walk
    to the

diner in Red Cloud, where he sits at the long table, the air
warm with coffee and conversation. And I remember
    memory

a book and a place where it was read, and how little
books are compared to bodies tossed overboard from
    coffin ships.

III

'Tzu-kung said, "If you had a piece of beautiful jade here,
would you put it away safely in a box or would you sell
it for a good price?' The Master said, 'Of course I would
sell it. Of course I would sell it. All I am waiting for is
the right offer."'
    – Confucius *Analects*

Late April in Nebraska: Dinnertime

Late April. Three times already
I've put away my winter coat.

This evening a crowd of coyote
kids some of them mine are
sheltered on the porch and howling.

A white cat with mismatched eyes
in the process of being adopted
is waiting for me, and I'm singing

along to whatever's on the radio
and dancing with the first cousin
of the bride at a wedding in

Co. Tipperary and not concerned
about this cat's can of 'Friskies.'

I'm cooking carrots, ziti,
and the shrimp for which Nebraska
has yet to establish a reputation.

If you watch from the potholed alley
behind the house, you'll see me tending
these daily masterpieces for my wife

and kids with wooden spoons & pots
& pans & glass doors open to the world.

Late April evening in Nebraska,
a wind shuffling down from Canada
before the call goes out to eat.

The Field, the Sea

My townie hands – like lit bulbs
in a shop window on Rafter Street –
froze in the wind blowing across
the old farmer's potato drills

to arrive at the ditch was beyond me.

When I could no longer count my buckets
I walked to the van where he puffed
at his pipe and tapped with his stick
among the flasks & ham sandwiches.

He described
my grandfather's genius with cars.

I cannot be a farmer,
could never fill the enormous prairie
with my weak prayers.

I listen for the Dodge St.
traffic, adjust the blinds each morning
to give light to my daughter's cactus
her red wine parka on my chair,
our room of videos, books, spotted beanbags.

A few weeks ago
I strode across the tarmac
of Seattle/Tacoma airport towards a
waiting commuter plane.

Quality of light
weight of air, temperature
beating of my heart, moisture of my skin.
I had to stop one single moment to pinch myself.

Blair, Nebraska

Magic. The long freight trains
of the Union Pacific Railroad crossing
the road at the edge of town. Air brakes,
dong, dong, dong rhythms, and the final
grand shriek of the whistle bringing me back
to the imagined America the years have stripped away.

Cornfields. At night the stalks extend into domes
covering the town. Dew falls onto the roofs
of houses, beads of moonlight seep through.

Twilight. Crimson strokes across a
deadening sky. You cannot breathe.
A dead grass snake on the sidewalk,
a parked white *Lumina* on Lincoln St.

Thunderstorms. The children stand on chairs
in front of us viewing 'Night on Bald Mountain.'
My daughter smells of rain, she is the rain
my hands light on her shoulders till the wind
blows off and we hear in the distance 'Ave Maria'
and watch ghostly figures march into darkness
across the streets, the railway line, into
those fields hidden from car lights and naked eyes.

The Prairie. Is what describes your secret. Jane
Smiley calls you vast and subtle, uneager to
display yourself. This town the size of my
hometown you surround, in my son's soft sleep
I hear your sweep across the distances of
Nebraska the mysterious romance of home.

The Rock Called

the submarine is shark-shaped.
Gulls and waves drive us back
till on the ebb we mount, then
crouch against the smashing sea.
Up periscope, fire torpedoes.

Victoria, British Columbia

Green, dogwood trees, gnarled oaks
driftwood at Oak Bay. I am far
north in winter again where daylight
swiftly evaporates, where morning is
as sodden as the Parliament grass.
I have come to an outpost of empire
to encounter familiar separations
and eat familiar dishes. I remember
your long fingers like sticks in the
stones, your children asleep, my first
view of the Pacific in Mexico when we
lay exhausted and full of songs:
how this ocean makes me want to weep.
I think of the hard air of the prairie
which lurks in each winter maple &
the brilliant light of early morning.
I am soft-skinned, broken-kneed
oar-buried, man-of-war, Irish.

Early Nights on the Prairie

Dust rises into the air
from behind a moving car,

a man on a porch on a
rocking chair on a

summer evening on Lincoln St.
(pipe smoke above his head)
watching his wife walk

across the yard, a child
with straight white teeth

whose eyes are obscured
by the peak of a baseball hat,

early night – hopes like whistles
reach out across the prairie.

My daughter and son allow
their limbs touch on a swing

in a new house examining this
almost silent red road parade.

A Prairie Poet!

I say to you:
'I'd like to
write prairie
dogs and Sandhill
cranes but I don't
feel comfortable:
I just blew in
from the East
four years ago.'

The Muse
of Brooklyn
answers,

'this kind
of technicality
never stopped you
before, Pal,'
& she raised
her chin &
stuck out her
tongue, before
giving me the
finger.
'Now get
outta here.'

This is
how I became a
prairie poet.

'An' ya go home to
Wexford whenever
ya get the chance

a prairie poet,
Yeah, right.'

Where Your Cousins Are Sleeping

In another corner of the world
narrow room waves breaking into

their dreams of carnival clangings
an hour on the beach. Oisín &

Naoise sleeping, a small square
window lets in a breeze from the

west which tempers sleeping happy
in the heatwave of this summer,

todays and tomorrows are rich
enough for dreaming. Tell us

about everything we have missed
my children on the porch in-between

bites of chicken and salad how rich
we are in nephews & cousins, how rich

those towels on the beach at Ardamine
held down by grey stones smoothed by

Irish sea. I won't forget those
boys and girls whose dreaming this

evening I'm not privileged to
view. We know this room and beach,

they say, and that music from a tape
recorder blowing across the grass

'I'll Tell Me Ma,' 'The Boys of Wexford,'
'Seán South from Garryowen.'

Yes, I say, and your mother put
her book aside one night and sat

stock-still listening to the sea
in the room where your cousins are sleeping.

Great Sand Dunes/Colorado

We drive
on the flat roads
of a high plateau

in the Rocky Mountains
to the huge dunes.

Twelve children
on their knees

bright hats like
sails on the water.

Smelling the sea
I fall among them

scooping water
to my face easing

my jeans into heavy
sand where once

the bottom-feeding
flounder ruled supreme

here in the Rockies
at the seaside.

Crossing Paths

'Does the city, any city, need Hope Church?
Does America need people on the land?'
– Kathleen Norris, *Dakota: A Spiritual Geography*

You left the many textured splendid cacophonies of New
York City to study climate in Lemmon, South Dakota.
You dimmed the lights, turned the music down, made of
the weather forecast a bright fable. The winds becoming
your *Daily News*.

You speak of how we are dulled by communication,
lured off the Interstate by the distant dust to the west.

What's left, I wonder, after the military and farmers
have departed the Dakotas? In the monasteries you
join the monks in their work of loading silos, now
decommissioned, with loaves of bread. The Cold War
ends in prayer. Leonid Brezhnev said to Jimmy Carter
'God will never forgive us if we don't....' Empty prairie
and high plains, nerve centres of the Cold War.

When I was a kid we crossed the path and entered the
monastery church by a side door to hear Sunday Mass.
In those days, the big groups were Led Zeppelin and
Deep Purple. The monks chanted beautifully, but I was
thinking of women and beer. The Easter break was days
away &

early light entered through the fogged windows of
the dormitory, dreamworlds which could never be
recovered whole.

49

The huge door of the school was bolted hard behind me,
that day I left the spirit-world for the honeyed land of
flesh and rock 'n roll,

mid-June and headed for the longest day when I passed
over the cattle bars, joined the main road, and left the
Midlands.

This morning I head across the plains toward the desert
by mounds & posts & churches thinking of Auden in
Barcelona listening for the chapel bells which did not toll,
hearing children howling in an orphanage, a gunman at a
front door in Belfast looking for your Da.

Each day after school, my son checks his garden for those
small signs which give us hope, leaps in high excitement
when a shoot appears, sits on a length of wood feasting
on lettuce leaves, admiring his purple sage, oregano,
and thyme.

A Climbing Wave

She raises her arms above a climbing wave
like a movie star removes her drown-ded shirt

Above and behind her black hair
wallows buckthorn, grass,
asbestos and tin-roofed houses,

a long waning shadow

& Doyle's field where we jump
hay bales before crossing
the Melling Road

She fiddles buttons and straps
so self-assured, as I float on
the backwash watching her breasts
heave, unable to hold my ground.

Kearney & Platte & Cranes

I'll drive west to seek the crane voice river with the lovely
name and your poets, Nebraska,

who read among the coloured walls of Kearney & Zeami
your performances loaded as the large, empty corn fields
in the car beside me. You know it all: I have come to
learn this river and this land.

Over the wave paths of this ancient sea with the light of
the setting sun in the waves

clouds like banners which obey the ancient rules of the
Interstate keeping the world at 75 rocking the voids of the
westward sky.

When the moon rises the distant mountains are framed &
numbers emerge clearer & bluer from the dashboard.
Great waters toss and toss, the grey waves soak the sky,

for ten million years they have been coming to the Platte,
the Sandhill cranes.

Iron Mountain Road

'Take Iron Mountain Road,'
the clerk in the gift shop said

this iron-red surface
into a forest cut
out of fairyland:
soft walls at the
edges early June
retreating fog the
same road above
as below turned like
liquorice in an
infant's hand.

Three pig-tail bridges on the famous
Iron Mountain Road were designed by
Senator Peter Norbeck to fully enjoy
the natural beauty of the surrounding
area. The tunnels on Iron Mountain
Road were positioned to frame Mt.
Rushmore.

Black Hills, South Dakota.
Photo Courtesy of Jack Riordain
c Rushmore Photo 1992
Rapid City, SD 57701
Printed in Canada.

Iron Mountain Road
Pig-Tail Bridge
United States of America

tyres crushing bones
white station wagon on this red
ascending road which fights pebble
by pebble, tree by tree
these brittle holy hills

we Irish know these bitter
woes and we sent our bitter
hardened hands to
build the railroad but
little did we know and
little did we care
our own despair enormous

and so I have taken
Iron Mountain Road and
found great spirits frightened
Great Faces Great Places.

On the Red River Bridge

Great sea
high
semi-arid
southern Colorado

bison
cattle raid

Red River
Slaney
at Edermine

pinõn pine
sage, dock
leaf &
heather

rattlesnakes
& saints

Sangré de Cristo
my feet on
the mesa

my voice is yours
America
your land mine.

Prospects/South Dakota

I follow this mighty road

while you talk of steak
and sleep in Chamberlain

hard by the Missouri River

Yellow Band

I

A Yellow Band

A yellow band floats like a sail boat timidly at anchor
near the lifeboat in the harbour. I saw it coming from
Chicago by airplane that first time when temperatures
had climbed, snow melted and grass daydreamed in one
yellow midwinter pall. Where will it be tonight, I hear
my brother say, The Bayview or Kinsella's? Wind
blowing from Wales onto the carnival lights onto the
water – boat rattles, wind chimes of America.

II

We favour the simple expression of the complex thought.
We are for a large shape.... We are for flat forms because
they destroy illusion and reveal truth.

Once after dark I slipped out of bed and went outside to
the corner of the garden where my wife and children had
been turning the ground in preparation for planting our
geraniums – they had been inside all winter by a glass
door for visitors to fall over on their way to the toilet. By
nature, I'm a kitchen person – preferring pots and pans to
rakes and spades. Like my grandfather with tobacco, I
rolled the soil on my left palm moving my tight-wrapped
fingers counter clock wise. I opened my shirt, spread
earth on my chest, under my armpits, down my jeans.
I sat down, fingers pressed to my nose, soldered and

57

grounded. Under the wide, clear sky of early May, I grew cold and drew the garden hose into the garage to wash myself down. I hoped that none of the neighbours had been watching.

III

We assert that the subject is crucial and only that subject matter is valid which is tragic and timeless. That is why we profess spiritual kinship with primitive and archaic art.

In Lincoln, I worried about the weather as I entered the museum, imagined ice-coated poles and wires falling on the kitchen as you waited for me to hear your stories. That day I found the centre of the prairie on an upstairs wall painted by an immigrant from Russia. It was what I had been searching for since County Wexford had given me no language to describe this unfixed loneliness outside my door. I recall the train leaving Enniscorthy, going north by the Slaney then frozen – an oak tree in the centre of a field, a herd of cows, a red Fiat headed for town – then moving on again toward Ferns.

IV

Thus, the yellow band of the title is hardly a band at all, but a zone of intense colour that feathers into bands above and below of a rich orange. All three strata of intensity fade, close to the framing edge, into a surround of thinly brushed pink.

We grow into houses and take them over. Replace the
departed's bits and pieces with books and sticks of
furniture. A piece of Badger Hill pottery has found its
homestead in a Nebraska kitchen, become one centre of
what surrounds it, just as a girl from across the street
rings our bell, calls out for the new kids to play with her.
I saw the painting, read the booklet in a plastic pouch on
the wall, and asked the curator to make me a copy.
Yellow Band is beautiful, I said. She agreed and made me
feel good about myself as an art critic. Why are you
interested in it, she asked? Beyond yellow and orange, I
couldn't say though I sensed in it some distant field
where the corn rolled over with the wind/porch lights
and cable television (*The Cartoon Network*)/a woman or
man in a car on a dark evening who has just now found
these bright spots/radio tuned to the station with the
most accurate weather report/hearing a country 'n
western song about going home or being lost in Texas/a
movement from static to children's voices. But I could
not say these words to her or look her in the face.

V

*In 1964, eight years after Mark Rothko painted the Sheldon
Gallery's 'Yellow Band,' the artist shrouded his studio skylight
with a parachute, creating a dimly lit gloom he found ideal for
his work.*

This morning I walked by the blue and white homes of
registered Republicans wondering how anybody could
be like that. I saw Newt's face in every rose in Memorial
Park. Still, earlier before breakfast I walked about the

house opening blinds and curtains knowing that through
the years a painting had become the essence of a place it
had never been meant to represent, that I could become
an art critic after all, if someone would just give me a
start. I saw drumlins between Red Cloud and the Kansas
line, and sat on the grass at the end of the prom watching
the Urrin and Slaney converge from red to orange to
yellow. I heard music blaring in the Abbey Square.
I have eggs and bacon to prepare.

VI

Yellow Band

It was chance which brought us here. The movers placed
the flat boxes in the hallway and after spitting on their
hands asked me if I'd play them *Black 47* to pick up bits
and pieces while the children were at school, time kept
by car alarms and a family from China eager to inspect
our rooms. How we left New York, our canvas changing
its colours like a Galapagos bird. Upstairs the sleeping
children, I sit at the kitchen table where I have always
sat with newspapers and a pot of tea, each evening
commemorating what has passed. It's silent, snow falls
into rectangles. Look through the doors if you will – full
length and glass – locate in deep shades some immigrant
myth. I must cut the dead tree in the backyard, clear the
ground under the buckled flagstone, make it even for the
children on their bikes. I have come from damp grass to
dry air to scrape film from formica, freed by exile to walk
out into the fresh renewing rectangle of a winter storm.
Who can say to me you don't belong – pictures hung,
boxes folded in the basement.

Three

Magic Barrel Man

A daughter carrying books emerges from the subway into
the smoky evening. Blue lights over the liquor store,
men and cigarettes. A bouncing ball, Jackie Robinson.

The first five years in the New World. Brooklyn, New York.

Two men sit in an apartment, the younger teaching his
elder words to give substance to the death of the family,
Manhattan humming beyond the window panes.

The magic barrel man is my father, I'll have you know.

Cobblers, rabbis, and matchmakers waiting and weeping
while the bride is stripped bare. To taste heat in my
mouth and feel less pain. It is not possible to be unhappy
in America.

In Inwood, an old tailor has a heart attack on the side-
walk while a broad-shouldered youth runs off with the
cash from his shop. And I am across the street watching
the fracas like a man reading a book, or a foreigner watch-
ing a movie depicting life in America.

How your stories, Bernard Malamud, have made the city
less confusing, menorahs in windows and lights on trees
reduced finally to a normal size as it was years ago when
at the age of seven I was seen walking across Enniscorthy
wearing my Éamon De Valera glasses for the first time.

I listen to the old tailor while my kids watch him draw liquorice from the money drawer, and when they settle in to hear him make the Singer hum, I imagine him and me huddled in the corner of the shop seeking each other's warmth – father & son, teacher & student. Immigrants sitting in luminous silence: wealthy & wise & weeping.

But I hear the tailor's children have come and led him to the suburbs, just as he had led his brothers & sisters out of Germany, raising them as father & mother in America. Soon the travel agency offering package tours to the Sandals resort in Jamaica will absorb his shop, and there won't be a thing remaining but words on a page.

I write these words & kiss your foreheads, Fathers.

Floors, Fences, Paint

We dig each hole, place each pole, add
ground and stones as working side by
side we painted walls – coat after coat
on new blocks of white emulsion, your
wireless coming in loud and clear. You
hold your level as I lean on a timber
plank above the wobbly slowly setting
concrete. Your corners must be perfect
whereas I will follow Darwin and allow
the floor-to-be to find a level of its own
in this room where many times you ran
a pencil from forehead to wall to gauge
my growth. We sit in a thick dust
with uncleanable hands and ham sandwiches,
outside your roses cut against winter blown
off the Irish Sea, fallen into a tired
camaraderie, turn off the tripswitch, load
up the car, begin the journey home.

Bare Meadows of Summer

The bare meadows of the Slaney are yellow dry

the bacon factory upstream of the old bridge is history
so washed of blood

the Abbey Square's become a freeway joining Wexford
to the Treaty of Rome &

a piece of the felled Cotton Tree decorates a coffee table
in my house in Omaha

the United Irishmen were buoyed by the red-hot weather
– where the estuary ends the tide turns –

but the weather broke in '98, today in County Wexford
90, in Nebraska, 104

you wait on Dodge St. for the bus. I see the ghost of
Miles Byrne who never returned from France retreating
to a pub

from jackhammer, lorry, helmet, chain-saw, dust – this
county council narrative –

flesh burned in the courthouse & General Lake & dying
for Ireland, dying in Wexford, to be

stranded in some airport on the first leg as the prom's
chestnuts root under the desolation of the sewage scheme

the river is low

a couple stumbles hand-in-hand up Castle Hill to the
torn-up Market Sq.

the sun goes down on on Oliver Sheppard, Fr. Murphy,
the Croppy Boy.

Till Edges Curve

Once in the hall
in Courtown Harbour
she moved close enough
for me to know she
had been swimming,

she was
a city street
festooned with shops
& folks, water
gathered into air,

then she moved away
to laugh on Donal
Conlon's shoulder.

I have filled these spaces
till edges
curve, roads lapse
low under primrose
and gorse. Empty
as a beach &
everything as
she was a time, a
rock, a sod, a
young woman at a
Sergio Leone film
I feared approaching.

The West

I run but the prairie runs faster
my shadow drifts into the burning
end: the western landscape promises
on another day arrival at water.

Native American Festival/Inwood Park

Our ladies of coolers and Spanish rice,
of *Heineken, Budweiser,* and children
spreadeagled across my vision blending
brown-eyed into burnt grass & chestnut
trees. The essence of Sunday mothers
with whom I travel the subway on field
trips with the class, whose husbands
play soccer. In the Museum of the American
Indian, Ms. Moch reminds the children of
how the painters stereotype Native
Americans while the other teachers
laugh. At the end of the soccer field
Manhattan was sold for trinkets to the
Dutch. Today, at the Native American
Festival while drummers and sean nós
singers rest, Pete Seeger sings 'This
Land Is Your Land. This Land Is My
Land' to forty people. I look at his
brand new *Nikes* as he sings, holding
my daughter at her waist on a corner
of the stage, chilled by his heroic
life, if not by his banjo playing.
Beyond outboard engines of Sunday
afternoon Indy drivers, pedal to the
metal, parody of the parable of walking
on the water of the channel joining
the Hudson and Harlem rivers, a
flattened portero and referee's
whistle, crab fishermen pulling pots

across an estuary bottom treacherous
as blackcurrant *Jello* and muck. When the
drumming and singing resume we join
the circle, follow the line. 'This
Land Was Made for You and Me.' The
players have retreated from the field,
fathers sit all golden among their lovers.

Father & Son: Nebraska

When we got home after the holidays
the streets near the Market Square
seemed dimmed and ceilings dropped
by the end of the summer though
it was warm still.

But we had known:
for a week lights had gone on earlier
and voices fainter as girls made
their way by the cliffwalk to
Joe's Cafe and the coloured lights
of Courtown Harbour.

We were lying in
our beds reading while mothers
and aunts played rummy and poker.

After games on the putting green,
I drank my coke, watched
Dublin girls come through the door,
and played 'Yellow Submarine' on the
juke box so often that Joe plugged out
the machine and turned on the Light Programme.

My son at the kitchen table has
the little streets, chippers and
slot machines memorised.

How come,
he says, that kids can play the
slot machines in Courtown but are
not allowed inside the casinos
on the Missouri River?

In a photo
on the wall, his mother stands in
sweatshirt and jacket watching us swim.

For him the water is warm. His
grandparents' house his own.

Today
in 'Famous Footwear' a saleswoman
led him across the floor to where
the grown-up sizes were displayed.
This evening I remind him of
how big he is.

I prefer children's
shoes he says and roots for a CD to play.
The sea enters his view of the street,
evening falls, and in mid-March
he walks to the living room to plug-in
Christmas lights taped above the windows
which I will not remove.

I say the first
horse I backed was Meadow Court in Breen's
little bookie office with money advanced
by my babysitter when I was about your age.

The bulbs are coming up, he says. Soon, he says,
and stops. He knows I'm listening not for
what he has to say but eyes closed for
his timbré which tells me how it was to
lie in bed in summer, the sea not a quarter
mile away. Let's go out for ice-cream, he says.

Rooftops & Illusions

*'Towns are the illusion that things hang together somehow,
my pear, your winter.'*
  – Anne Carson, *Plainwater*

I sweep a flat space among the many-levelled sloping roofs
of this grey town. Slate and felt. Cars parked from St.
Aidan's down Main St. I hear on the wire that Jesus will
save us, that the cathedral restorations are simply gorgeous.

In her studio on the Market Sq. Mrs. Carty fills in the
edges of a photo the camera lost from scratchings in her
lap – communion girls. Blue skies, deep-red missals,
puffs of cloud.

Wildflowers are growing out of the walls, the gutters are
weighted with moss. White dots on the grey crown of
the Atheneum, the domino roofs of Slaney St. I touch
your knees & smell your breath as blood flows from
your orifices into the Slaney. You whisper dissolution,
departed children.

At seventeen I lay in bed hearing – prayers under bunting
& bridges for the Sacred Heart – reading *Down All the
Days*. I was thinking about the walkers stuck on the hills
in white dresses/sashes, waiting for the marching to
resume so I might continue with the rhythm of my reading.

To know I suppose one day I have longed forever to
describe to you. Childhood was a day when only
the surfaces counted, when we found the goalposts in
murky water near the Mill Field and made plans for
retrieving them.

When we stripped in the heavy night air under wild
fuschia and stars and watched cars come and go on the
Wexford Road. We are easily replaced and forgotten,
so skies and rivers are what we have learned to call
discourse. I am one man – you need to know this – grey
rooftop & water, undissolved by absence, crossing the old
bridge from the Shannon to the other side of town.